Handy Minnesota Genealogy Handbook

Gary L. Morris

©2015 Gary L. Morris

ISBN-13: 978-1507837153

ISBN-10: 1507837151

Table of Contents

Notes

Genealogical Research in Minnesota

There are many genealogical records and resources available for tracing your family history in Minnesota. Because there are so many records held at many different locations, tracking down the records for your ancestor can be an ominous task. Don't worry though, we know just where they are, and we'll show you which records you'll need, while helping you to understand:

1. What they are
2. Where to find them
3. How to use them

These records can be found both online and off, so we'll introduce you to online websites, indexes and databases, as well as brick-and-mortar repositories and other institutions that will help with your research in Minnesota. So that you will have a more comprehensive understanding of these records, we have provided a brief history of the "North Star State" to illustrate what type of records may have been generated during specific time periods. That information will assist you in pinpointing times and locations on which to focus the search for your Minnesota ancestors and their records.

A Brief History of Minnesota

Native American tribes the Dakota, Chippewa, and Ojibwa had long inhabited the lands now known as Minnesota before the arrival of the first Europeans around 1650. In 1679 the area was claimed for France by Daniel Greysolon, Sieur Duluth. The area was sparsely settled by French fur traders and missionaries who established settlements at Fort Antoine in 1686, and Fort St. Charles in 1731.

The French and Indian Wars saw the French defeated and the land west of the Mississippi ceded to Spain in 1762, the region east of the Mississippi ceded to Great Britain in 1763. There was little disruption to Minnesota life during the Revolutionary War, and as fur traders continued to settle the area, the North West Company built a major fur-trading post at Grand Portage. The fur trade flourished until after the War of 1812 when an act was passed by the United States Congress curbing British participation in the lucrative industry.

The part of Minnesota east of the Mississippi had become part of the Northwest Territory in 1787, while most of the western part was acquired by the United States in the Louisiana Purchase of 1803. In 1805, while searching for the source of the Mississippi River, Lieutenant Zebulon Pike concluded a treaty with a band of Dakota Indians for two pieces of land bordering the River. It was on this land that the construction of Fort Snelling was completed in 1820, a settlement that was to serve as as a key frontier outpost in the northwest and the principal center of civilization in Minnesota for years to come.

A series of treaties between the American government and the local Native American tribes transferred large areas of land to the United States. These treaties opened up the land to farming, lumbering, and settlement, but ended the profitable relationship between the Indians and fur traders. Permanent settlements such as St. Paul and St. Anthony (modern day Minneapolis) were established and in 1849 Minnesota became a separate territory.

In 1851 St. Paul became the capital of Minnesota, and by 1857 the population had reached more than 150,000. Minnesota was granted statehood on May 11, 1858, and the fast growing Republican Party seized political control of the state. The Republican majority helped Abraham Lincoln into office as president in 1860, and when Civil War broke out Minnesota sent over 20,000 plus troops to fight for the union cause.

In 1862 war broke out with the Native American Dakota tribe who had become grieved by the loss of their land and dissatisfied with life on the reservations. The murder of five white settlers by four young Dakota Indians ignited a bloody uprising in which more than 300 whites and an unknown number of Indians were killed. In the aftermath, 38 Dakota captives were hanged and the Dakota remaining in Minnesota were removed to reservations in Nebraska. Meanwhile, the Ojibwa were relegated to reservations on remnants of their former lands.

The year 1862 also saw Minnesota's first railroad open with ten miles of track joining St. Anthony (Minneapolis) and St. Paul. By 1867, the Twin Cities were connected with Chicago by rail; in the early 1870s, tracks crossed the prairie all the way to the Red River Valley. The railroads brought settlers, many from Scandinavia and Germany, and they, in turn, grew produce for the trains to carry back to the cities of the east. The railroads soon ushered in an era of large-scale commercial farming.

Important Dates in Minnesota History

1680– Sparsely settled by French fur traders and missionaries.

1763 – Ceded from France to Great Britain

1774 – Part of Quebec

1783 – Area east of the Mississippi ceded from Great Britain to United States

1787 – Part of Northwest Territory

1803 – Area west of the Mississippi acquired by US in the Louisiana Purchase

1820 – Fort Snelling established

1830 – Part of Michigan territory

1836 – Part of Wisconsin Territory

1849 – Minnesota made a separate territory

1858 – Statehood

1862 – Dakota Rebellion

Famous Battles Fought in Minnesota

Ni Civil War battles were fought in Minnesota, but over 20,000 men from the state fought for the Union cause. You can find links to their records in the **Military Records** part of this handbook, and below links to the records of those regiments who fought in the **Dakota Uprising**.

These battle accounts that exist can be very effective in uncovering the military records of your ancestor. They can tell you what regiments fought in which battles, and often include the names and ranks of many officers and enlisted men.

Dakota Uprising:
http://www.startribune.com/opinion/commentaries/191468751.html

Common Minnesota Genealogical Issues and Resources to Overcome Them

Boundary Changes: Boundary changes are a common obstacle when researching Minnesota ancestors. You could be searching for an ancestor's record in one county when in fact it is stored in a different one due to historical county boundary changes.

The **Atlas of Historical County Boundaries** can help you to overcome that problem. It provides a chronological listing of every boundary change that has occurred in the history of Minnesota.

Atlas of Historical County Boundaries:
http://publications.newberry.org/ahcbp/documents/MN_Consolidate d_Chronology.htm#Consolidated_Chronology

Name Changes: Surname changes, variations, and misspellings can complicate genealogical research. It is important to check all spelling variations. Soundex, a program that indexes names by sound, is a useful first step, but you can't rely on it completely as some name variations result in different Soundex codes. The surnames could be different, but the first name may be different too. You can also find records filed under initials, middle names, and nicknames as well, so you will need to **get creative with surname variations** and spellings in order to cover all the possibilities. For help with surname variations read our instructional article on **How to Use Soundex**.

get creative with surname variations:
http://obituarieshelp.org/blog/?p=634

How to Use Soundex: http://obituarieshelp.org/blog/?p=505

Minnesota Genealogical Organizations and Archives

Genealogical resources include not only records, but the organizations that house them, or can direct you to them. These institutions include: *Archives, Libraries, Genealogical Societies, Family History Centers, Universities, Churches, and Museums.*

Following are links to their websites, their physical addresses, and a summary of the records you can find there.

Archives and Libraries

Minnesota State Archives – vital records indexes, state census, immigration resources, family histories, newspaper collection and more

345 W. Kellogg Blvd.
St. Paul, Minnesota 55102-1906
Phone: (651) 296-6126

Minnesota State Archives: http://www.mnhs.org/genealogy/

National Archives Great Lake Region (Chicago) – court records, naturalization records, Chinese exclusions, Native American records and more

7358 South Pulaski Road
Chicago, IL 60629
Telephone: 312-581-7816

National Archives Great Lake Region (Chicago):
http://www.archives.gov/chicago/

Minnesota Discovery Center - extensive collection of records dealing with the string of towns that extends about 200 miles east to west across St. Louis County and other counties. This was a mining area where many immigrants were employed.

Highway 169 West
P. O. Box 392
Chisholm, MN 55719
Telephone: 1-800-372-6437
Fax: 218-254-5235

Minnesota Discovery Center: http://mndiscoverycenter.com/

Cloquet Public Library – historical newspapers, county records, many records from the State Archives on microfilm including; census records, records from the Swedish National Archives, and a variety of other genealogical resources

320 14th St.
Cloquet, MN 55720
Tel: 218-879-1531
Email: cloquet.library@gmail.com

Cloquet Public Library:
http://www.cloquet.lib.mn.us/genealogy.html

Minnesota Genealogical and Historical Societies

Genealogical and historical societies have access to extensive catalogs of genealogical data. They are also able to offer expert guidance for genealogical researchers.

Minnesota Genealogical Society – church records, county resources, and many other genealogical resources for tracing Minnesota ancestors

1185 Concord St. N
Suite 218
South St. Paul, MN 55075-1150
Tel: 651 455-9057

Minnesota Genealogical Society: **http://www.mngs.org/**

Minnesota Historical Society - local, county, school district, city, and state government records, historical newspapers

345 Kellogg Boulevard W.
St. Paul, MN 55102-1906
Telephone: 651-296-2143
Fax: 651-297-7436

Minnesota Historical Society: http://sites.mnhs.org/library/

West Central Minnesota Research Center – University of Minnesota, Morris – Native American records, oral histories, business and cooperative records, personal papers, journals and periodicals, rural school records.

600 East 4th Street
Morris, Minnesota 56267
Toll Free: (888)-866-3382, Tel: (320)-589-6035

West Central Minnesota Research Center:
http://www.morris.umn.edu/library/collections/researchcenter/

Northwest Minnesota Historical Center – Minnesota State University, Moorehead - newspapers, business records, correspondence, diaries, oral interviews, photographs, and other genealogical and historical resources

Livingston Lord Library
Moorhead State University
Moorhead, MN 56563
Telephone: 218-236-2345
Fax: 218-299-5924

Northwest Minnesota Historical Center:
http://web.mnstate.edu/archives/NorthwestMN/

Additional Minnesota Genealogical Resources

Minnesota Mailing Lists

Mailing lists are internet based facilities that use email to distribute a single message to all who subscribe to it. When information on a particular surname, new records, or any other important genealogy information related to the mailing list topic becomes available, the subscribers are alerted to it. Joining a mailing list is an excellent way to stay up to date on Minnesota genealogy research topics. Rootsweb have an extensive listing of **Minnesota Mailing Lists** on a variety of topics.

Minnesota Mailing Lists:
http://lists.rootsweb.ancestry.com/index/usa/MN/misc.html

Minnesota Message Boards

A message board is another internet based facility where people can post questions about a specific genealogy topic and have it answered by other genealogists. If you have questions about a surname, record type, or research topic, you can post your question and other researchers and genealogists will help you with the answer. Be sure to check back regularly, as the answers are not emailed to you. The Minnesota message boards at **Rootsweb** are completely free to use.

Rootsweb:
http://boards.rootsweb.com/localities.northam.usa.states/mb.ashx

Minnesota Newspapers and Periodicals

Many genealogy periodicals and historical newspapers contain reprinted copies of family genealogies, transcripts of family Bible records, information about local records and archives, census indexes, church records, queries, land records, obituaries, court records, cemetery records, and wills. The following sites have historical Minnesota newspapers and periodicals that you can search online or on-site.

Minnesota State Archives – Minnesota newspapers with dates ranging from 1849 to the present day

345 W. Kellogg Blvd.
St. Paul, Minnesota 55102-1906
Phone: (651) 296-6126

Minnesota State Archives:
http://sites.mnhs.org/library/content/newspaper-collection

GenealogyBank.com – free searchable database of Minnesota newspaper archives, 1849–1923

GenealogyBank.com:
http://www.genealogybank.com/gbnk/newspapers/explore/USA/Minnesota/

Library of Congress Digital Newspaper Directory – free searchable database of historical U.S. newspapers dating from 1690-present

Library of Congress Digital Newspaper Directory:
http://chroniclingamerica.loc.gov/search/titles/

The Online Books Page – links to historical Minnesota books and periodicals available for viewing online, dating from mid-16th century

The Online Books Page: http://onlinebooks.library.upenn.edu

NewspaperArchive.com – largest online database of historical newspapers in the world.

NewspaperArchive.com: http://newspaperarchive.com/

Historical Minnesota Maps and Gazetteers

Maps are an integral part of genealogical research. They help us to locate landmarks, towns, cities, parishes, states, provinces, waterways and roads and streets. They also help us to determine when and where boundary changes might have taken place, and give us a visualization of the area we're researching in.

For locating place names, a gazetteer is the best possible resource for any genealogist. Gazetteers are also sometimes called "place name dictionaries", and can help you to locate the area in which you need to conduct research. Below are links to the maps and gazetteers for research in Minnesota.

Peabody GNIS Service – Minnesota:
http://peabody.research.yale.edu/cgi-bin/Query.GNIS?ST=Minnesota&SU=1

Color Landform Atlas – Minnesota:
http://fermi.jhuapl.edu/states/mn_0.html

1985 U.S. Atlas: http://www.livgenmi.com/1895/MN/

Minnesota Hometown Locator:
http://minnesota.hometownlocator.com/

Minnesota City Directories

City directories are similar to telephone directories in that they list the residents of a particular area. The difference though is what is important to genealogists, and that is they pre-date telephone directories. You can find an ancestor's information such as their street address, place of employment, occupation, or the name of their spouse. A one-stop-shop for finding city directories in Minnesota is the **Minnesota Online Historical Directories** which contains a listing of every available online historical directory related to Minnesota.

Minnesota Online Historical Directories:
https://sites.google.com/site/onlinedirectorysite/Home/usa/mn

Fold3 has Minneapolis directories from 1865 to 1871, and yearly 1873-1923, and St. Paul directories from 1863 to 1871, and yearly 1873-1924.

Fold3: http://www.fold3.com/category_116/

Minnesota Genealogical Records

Birth, Death, Marriage and Divorce Records – Also known as vital records, birth, death, and marriage certificates are the most basic, yet most important records attached to your ancestor. The reason for their importance is that they not only place your ancestor in a specific place at a definite time, but potentially connect the individual to other relatives. Below is a list of repositories and websites where you can find Minnesota vital records.

Minnesota Office of Vital Records – birth records from 1900 to present and death records from 1908 to present

P.O. Box 64975
St. Paul, MN 55164-0975
Tel: 651-201-5000

Minnesota Office of Vital Records:
http://www.health.state.mn.us/divs/chs/osr/

Minnesota State Archives – death certificates from 1908 to 2001, death cards from 1904 to 1907, birth records from 1900-1934, 2700 pre-1900 records

345 W. Kellogg Blvd.
St. Paul, Minnesota 55102-1906
Phone: (651) 296-6126

Minnesota State Archives: http://www.mnhs.org/genealogy/

Marriage and **Divorce** records are maintained by the **County Recorders**

County Recorders:
http://www.health.state.mn.us/divs/chs/osr/registrars.html

Family Search has the following indexes which can be searched online for free:

Minnesota, Birth Index, 1935-2002:
https://familysearch.org/search/collection/1949334

Minnesota, Births and Christenings, 1840-1980:
https://familysearch.org/search/collection/1680827

Minnesota, County Birth Records, 1863-1983:
https://familysearch.org/search/collection/1920099

Minnesota, County Marriages, 1860-1949:
https://familysearch.org/search/collection/1803974

Minnesota, Death Index, 1908-2002:
https://familysearch.org/search/collection/1937234

Minnesota, Death Records, 1866-1916:
https://familysearch.org/search/collection/1858352

Minnesota, Deaths and Burials, 1835-1990:
https://familysearch.org/search/collection/1680831

Minnesota, Divorce Index, 1970-1995:
https://familysearch.org/search/collection/1967743

Minnesota, Marriage Index, 1958-2001:
https://familysearch.org/search/collection/1949335

Minnesota, Marriages, 1849-1950:
https://familysearch.org/search/collection/1680832

Census Reports

Census records are among the most important genealogical documents for placing your ancestor in a particular place at a specific time. Like BDM records, they can also lead you to other ancestors, particularly those who were living under the authority of the head of household.

Federal census records for Minnesota exist from 1850–1930 and can be found at:

Minnesota State Archives – Census records from 1849, 1850, 1853, 1855, 1857, 1865, 1875, 1885, 1895, and 1905

345 W. Kellogg Blvd.
St. Paul, Minnesota 55102-1906
Phone: (651) 296-6126

Minnesota State Archives: http://people.mnhs.org/census/

National Archives – Federal census Schedules for all states, 1790-1940

8601 Adelphi Road
College Park, MD 20740-6001
Tel: 1-866-272-6272

National Archives: http://www.archives.gov/research/census/

The **Free Census Project** has transcribed many Minnesota indexes and new material is added daily

Free Census Project: http://usgwcensus.org/cenfiles/mn.htm

Access Genealogy – Minnesota county census records from 1870-1930

Access Genealogy:
http://www.accessgenealogy.com/census/minnesota-census-records.htm

African American Census Schedules Online – slave schedules, mortality schedules, slave-owners census

African American Census Schedules Online:
http://www.afrigeneas.com/aacensus/

Native Americans in Census Records (US National Archives):
http://www.archives.gov/research/census/native-americans/

Minnesota Church Records

Church and synagogue records are a valuable resource, especially for baptisms, marriages, and burials that took place before 1900. You will need to at least have an idea of your ancestor's religious denomination, and in most cases you will have to visit a brick and mortar establishment to view them.

Most church records are kept by the individual church, although in some denominations, records are placed in a regional archive or maintained at the diocesan level. Local Historical Societies are sometimes the repository for the state's older church records. Below are links archives that maintain church records, as well as a few databases that can be viewed online.

The **Family History Library** contains many church records from a variety of denominations on microfilm.

Family History Library:
http://familysearch.org/learn/wiki/en/Family_History_Library

Minnesota Genealogical Society – excerpts of Catholic records from the Archdiocese of St. Paul and Minneapolis

1185 Concord St. N
Suite 218
South St. Paul, MN 55075-1150
Tel: 651 455-9057

Minnesota Genealogical Society:
http://www.mngs.org/catholicstpaul.htm

The **Swenson Center at Augustana College** - collection of
Minnesota church records from most Minnesota counties that
include, Lutheran, Baptist, Evangelical, First Covenant, and a few
other denominational records

639 38th St.
Rock Island, Illinois 61201
Tel: 309-794-7000
Toll Free: 800-798-8100

Swenson Center at Augustana College:
https://www.augustana.edu/general-information/swenson-center-
/genealogy/church-records/minnesota

Central Repositories for Denominational Records

Church of Jesus Christ of Latter-day Saints (Mormons)

Early Mormon Church records for Minnesota can be found on film
located at the LDS Family History Library in Salt Lake City and can
be searched via the **Family History Library Catalog**

Family History Library Catalog:
https://familysearch.org/eng/Library/FHLC/frameset_fhlc.asp

Congregational

Congregational Library
14 Beacon Street
Boston, MA 02108
Phone: (617) 523-0470
Fax: (617) 523-0491

Congregational Library: http://www.14beacon.org/

Jewish

American Jewish Historical Society Library
2 Thornton Road
Waltham, MA 02453-7711
Phone: (781) 891-8110
Fax: (781) 899-9208
E-mail Address: ajhs@ajhs.org

American Jewish Historical Society Library: http://www.ajhs.org/

Lutheran

Evangelical Lutheran Church of America (ELCA), Region 3
2481 Como Avenue
St. Paul, MN 55108
Phone: (651) 641-3205

Evangelical Lutheran Church of America (ELCA), Region 3:
http://www.elca.org/Who-We-Are/Our-Three-
Expressions/Churchwide-Organization/Synodical-
Relations/Regions/Region-3.aspx

Presbyterian

Presbyterian Historical Society and Department of History
United Presbyterian Church USA
425 Lombard Street
Philadelphia, PA 19147-1516
Phone: (215) 627-1852
Fax: (215) 627-0509

Presbyterian Historical Society and Department of History:
http://www.history.pcusa.org/

Roman Catholic

Archdiocese of St. Paul
226 Summit Avenue
St. Paul, MN 55102
Phone: (651) 291-4400
Fax: (651) 290-1629

Archdiocese of St. Paul: http://www.archspm.org/index.php

Diocese of New Ulm
1400 6th Street N.
New Ulm, MN 56073-2099
Phone: (507) 359-2966
Fax: (507) 354-3667

Diocese of New Ulm: http://www.dnu.org/

Diocese of Crookston
1200 Memorial Drive
PO Box 610
Crookston, MN 56716
Phone: (218) 281-4533
Fax: (218) 281-3328

Diocese of Crookston: http://www.crookston.org/

Diocese of Duluth
2830 East 4th Street
Duluth, MN 55812
Phone: (218) 724-9111
Fax: (218) 724-1056

Diocese of Duluth: http://www.dioceseduluth.org/

Diocese of St. Cloud
214 South 3rd Avenue
St. Cloud, MN 56301
Phone: (320) 251-2340
Fax: (320) 251-0470
Mailing Address:
P.O. Box 1248
St. Cloud, MN 56302

Diocese of St. Cloud: http://stcdio.org/

Diocese of Winona
55 West Sanborn Street
Winona, MN 55987
Phone (507) 454-4643
Fax (507) 454-8106

Mailing Address:
P.O. Box 588
Winona, MN 55987

Diocese of Winona: http://www.dow.org/

Minnesota Military Records

More than 40 million Americans have participated in some time of war service since America was colonized. The chance of finding your ancestor amongst those records is exceptionally high. Military records can even reveal individuals who never actually served, such as those who registered for the two World Wars but were never called to duty.

Below are a number of links to websites and archives that contain Minnesota military records.

Minnesota Historical Society – vast array of Minnesota military records ranging from the Civil War to WWII, including the Dakota War conflict; covers every war that anyone from Minnesota ever fought in.

345 Kellogg Boulevard W.
St. Paul, MN 55102-1906
Telephone: 651-296-2143
Fax: 651-297-7436

Minnesota Historical Society:
http://www.mnhs.org/genealogy/family/genieguide/military.htm

U.S. National Archives – WWI Draft registration cards, casualties lists, WWI and WWII service records, Korean War records, Vietnam War records, Civil War and Spanish-American War records, and casualties lists.

U.S. National Archives:
http://www.archives.gov/research/military/veterans/online.html

US Department of Veterans Affairs Nationwide Gravesite Locator – includes information on veterans and their family members buried in veterans and military cemeteries having a government grave marker.

US Department of Veterans Affairs Nationwide Gravesite Locator: http://gravelocator.cem.va.gov/

You may also find your ancestor's military records in the following databases:

United States General Index to Pension Files, 1861-1934:
https://familysearch.org/search/collection/1919699

United States Index to Service Records, War with Spain, 1898:
https://familysearch.org/search/collection/1919583

United States Index to Indian Wars Pension Files, 1892-1926 – military pension records of soldiers who fought in the Indian Wars between 1817 and 1898

United States Index to Indian Wars Pension Files, 1892-1926:
https://familysearch.org/search/collection/1979427

United States Registers of Enlistments in the U.S. Army, 1798-1914 - index of men who enlisted in the United States Army, 1798-1914.

United States Registers of Enlistments in the U.S. Army, 1798-1914: https://familysearch.org/search/collection/1880762

United States Mexican War Pension Index, 1887-1926 - index to Mexican War pension files for service between 1846 and 1848

United States Mexican War Pension Index, 1887-1926:
https://familysearch.org/search/collection/1979390

Civil War Soldiers Service Records - Service records for both Union and Confederate soldiers indexed by soldier's name, rank, and unit.

Civil War Soldier Service Records:
http://go.fold3.com/civilwar_records/

Minnesota Cemetery Records

As convenient as it is to search cemetery records online, keep in mind that there are a few disadvantages over visiting a cemetery in person. They are:

1. Tombstone information is not always accurately transcribed
2. The arrangement of the graves in a cemetery can be crucial as family members are often buried next to each other or in the same grave. This arrangement is not always preserved in the alphabetical indexes that are found online.

With that information in mind, the following websites have databases that can be searched online for Minnesota Cemetery records.

Minnesota Genealogical Society – county cemetery records from across the state

1185 Concord St. N
Suite 218
South St. Paul, MN 55075-1150
Tel: 651 455-9057

Minnesota Genealogical Society:
http://www.mngs.org/resourcebyco1.htm

Minnesota Tombstone Transcription Project - death and burial records

Minnesota Tombstone Transcription Project:
http://www.usgwtombstones.org/minnesota/

African American Cemeteries Online – African American, slave, and Native American cemetery records

African American Cemeteries Online:
http://africanamericancemeteries.com/

Access Genealogy – huge database of Minnesota cemetery record transcriptions

Access Genealogy:
http://www.accessgenealogy.com/cemetery/minnesota-cemetery-records.htm

Find a Grave – over 100 million grave records can be searched on this site. Search can be conducted by name, location, or cemetery name.

Find a Grave: http://www.findagrave.com/

Interment.net - A free online database containing approximately 4 million cemetery records from around the world.

Interment.net: http://www.interment.net/

Billion Graves – as the name implies, you can search a billion records including headstone photos, transcriptions, cemetery records, and grave locations.

Billion Graves:
http://billiongraves.com/pages/search/index.php#cemetery

Minnesota Obituaries

Obituaries can reveal a wealth about our ancestor and other relatives. You can search our **Minnesota Newspaper Obituaries Listings** from hundreds of Minnesota newspapers online for free.

Minnesota Newspaper Obituaries Listings:
http://obituarieshelp.org/minnesota_newspaper_obituaries.html

Minnesota Wills and Probate Records

The documents found in a probate packet may include a complete inventory of a person's estate, newspaper entries, witness testimony, a copy of a will, list of debtors and creditors, names of executors or trustees, names of heirs. They can not only tell you about the ancestor you're currently researching, but lead to other ancestors.

Probate records in Minnesota are held by **County Probate Courts.** Other sources of Minnesota probate records are:

County Probate Courts:
http://www.health.state.mn.us/divs/chs/osr/registrars.html

Minnesota Historical Society – county court and probate records including; case files, will books, estate records, appointment books, insanity records and more

345 Kellogg Boulevard W.
St. Paul, MN 55102-1906
Telephone: 651-296-2143
Fax: 651-297-7436

Minnesota Historical Society:
http://www.mnhs.org/genealogy/family/genieguide/probate.htm

Family Search has the following index that can be searched online for free:

Minnesota, Will Records, 1849-1985:
https://familysearch.org/search/collection/1607922

Minnesota Immigration and Naturalization Records

The naturalization process generated many types of records, including petitions, declarations of intention, and oaths of allegiance. These records can provide family historians with information such as a person's birth date and place of birth, immigration year, marital status, spouse information, occupation, witnesses' names and addresses, and more.

Minnesota Historical Society – Alien Registration Records, Americanization Survey Cards, county Naturalization Records. Passenger and Immigration Lists Index, Czech Immigration Passenger Lists, German Immigrants: Lists of Passengers Bound from Bremen to New York, 1855-1862, 1863-1867, Germans to America: Lists of Passengers Arriving at U.S. Ports, Lists of Irish Immigrants Arriving at the Port of New York, 1846-1851, Russians: Migration from the Russian Empire: Lists of Passengers Arriving at the Port of New York, Swedes: Swedish Passenger Arrivals in New York, 1820-1850

345 Kellogg Boulevard W.
St. Paul, MN 55102-1906
Telephone: 651-296-2143
Fax: 651-297-7436

Minnesota Historical Society:
http://www.mnhs.org/genealogy/family/genieguide/immigration.htm

U.S. National Archives – Immigration and Naturalization records, 1787-1993

U.S. National Archives: http://www.archives.gov/research/guide-fed-records/groups/085.html

Family Search has the following index that can be searched online for free:

Minnesota, Naturalization Card Index, 1930-1988:
https://familysearch.org/search/collection/2120721

Minnesota Native American Records

Access Genealogy – Minnesota Native American census records, tribal histories, and much more

Access Genealogy:
http://www.accessgenealogy.com/native/minnesota-indian-tribes.htm

U.S. National Archives - information on American Indians who maintained their ties to Federally-recognized Tribes (1830-1970).

U.S. National Archives: http://www.archives.gov/research/native-americans/

Records of the Bureau of Indian Affairs (BIA):
http://www.archives.gov/research/guide-fed-records/groups/075.html

American Indians Records Repository - records dating from the 1700s including trust, education and other historic Indian Affairs records

American Indian Records Repository
Meritex Enterprises
17501 West 98th Street
Lenexa, KS 66219
Phone: 913-888-0601

American Indians Records Repository:
http://www.doi.gov/ost/records_mgmt/american-indian-records-repository.cfm

Missing Matriarchs – Resources for Researching Female Minnesota Ancestors

Looking for female ancestors requires an adjustment of how we view traditional records sources. A woman's identity was often under that of her husband, and often individual records for them can be difficult to locate. The following resources are effective in locating female ancestors in Minnesota where traditional records may not reveal them.

Bibliographies

- *Women's History in Minnesota: A Survey of Published Sources and Dissertations,* Jo Blatti (Minnesota Historical Society Press, 1993)
- *The Gold Rush Widows of Little Falls,* Linda Peavy and Ursula Smith (Minnesota Historical Society Press, 1990)
- *Women of Minnesota: Selected Biographical Essays,* Barbara Stuhler and Gretchen Kreuter (Minnesota Historical Society Press, 1977)
- *Dakota Women's Work,* Colette A. Hyman (Minnesota Historical Society Press, 2012)
- *In the Company of Women,* Bonnie Watkins and Nina Rothchild (Minnesota Historical Society Press, 1996)

Selected Resources for Minnesota Women's History

Upper Midwest Women's History Center
1110 Lincoln Avenue West
Fergus Falls, MN 56537

Minnesota Historical Society
345 Kellogg Boulevard
Saint Paul, MN 55012

Common Minnesota Surnames

The following surnames are among the most common in Minnesota and are also being currently researched by other genealogists. If you find your surname here, there is a chance that some research has already been performed on your ancestor.

Aitkin, Anoka, Becker, Beltrami, Benton, Big Stone, Blue Earth, Brown, Carlton, Carve, Cass, Chippewa, Chisago, Clay, Clearwater, Cook, Cottonwood, Crow Wing, Dakota, Dodge, Douglas, Faribault, Fillmore, Freeborn, Goodhue, Grant, Hennepin, Houston, Hubbard, Isanti, Itasca, Jackson, Kanabec, Kandiyohi, Kittson, Koochiching, Lac Qui Parle, Lake, Lake of Woods, Le Sueur, Lincoln, Lyon, Mahnomen, Marshall, Martin, McLeod, Meeker, MilleLacs, Morrison, Mower, Murray, Nicollet, Nobles, Norman, Olmsted, OtterTail, Pennington, Pine, Pipestone, Polk, Pope, Ramsey, RedLake, Redwood, Renville, Rice, Rock, Roseau, Scott, Sherburne, Sibley, Stearns, Steele, Stevens, StLouis, Swift, Todd, Traverse, Wabasha, Wadena, Waseca, Washington, Watonwan, Wilkin, Winona, Wright, Yellow Medicine

About the Author

Gary L. Morris worked from 2009 to 2014 as a professional researcher for a major player in the genealogy field. After tracing his family lineage back to 1683, he found that genealogy could be an expensive undertaking. As such, has decided to publish these helpful guides to share the valuable free information he has discovered during his career to help others trace their family lineages as inexpensively as possible. An avid genealogist himself, he hopes you will find this guide factual, thorough, helpful, and most of all, effective in helping you to find your family members.

Notes

Notes